BENDIS◊OEMING

Takio

Created by:
Brian Michael Bendis,
Michael Avon Oeming & Olivia Bendis
Executed by:
Brian Michael Bendis & Michael Avon Oeming
Layout Assists: Taki Soma
Colors: Nick Filardi
Letters & Production: Chris Eliopoulos
Editor: Jennifer Grunwald
Book Design: Patrick McGrath
Cover Design: Tim Daniel
Business Affairs: Alisa Bendis

PREVIOUSLY

Two sisters in a multi-racial, adoptive family are driving each other insane! Their overprotective mother makes them do everything together. They can't get away from each other!

But when a one-of-a-kind, once-in-a-lifetime accident gives them real-life superpowers, these two sisters become the first actual superheroes in the entire world. And it is awesome! Now the sisters have to get along, save the world and get home by six...or they are so grounded!

TAKIO 2. First printing 2013. Contains material originally published in magazine form as TAKIO VOL. 2 #1-4. ISBN# 978-0-7851-6553-8. Published by MARVEL WORLDWIDE, INC., a subsidiary of MARVEL ENTERTAINMENT, LLC. OFFICE OF PUBLICATION: 417 5th Avenue, New York, NY 10016. Copyright © 2012 and 2013 Jinxworld, Inc. All rights reserved. Takio, its logo design, and all characters featured in or on this issue and the distinctive names and likenesses thereof, and all related indicia are trademarks of Jinxworld, Inc. ICON and its logos are TM & © Marvel Characters, Inc. No similarity between any of the names, characters, persons, and/or institutions in this magazine with those of any living or dead person or institution is intended, and any such similarity that may exist is purely coincidental. $16.99 per copy in the U.S. and $18.99 in Canada (GST #R127032852); Canadian Agreement #40668537. **Printed in the U.S.A. Manufactured between 9/23/2013 and 11/4/2013 by R.R. DONNELLEY, INC.**, SALEM, VA, USA. by SHERIDAN BOOKS, INC., CHELSEA, MI, USA.

10 9 8 7 6 5 4 3 2 1

WHAT ARE YOU DOING??!!

FOR DONUTS!!

I'M NOT GOING TO JAIL FOR DONUTS!!

AAAIIIEEE!!!

TRY NOT TO MISS.

YEAH TRY NOT TO SUCK!

WHOAWAZAKI!

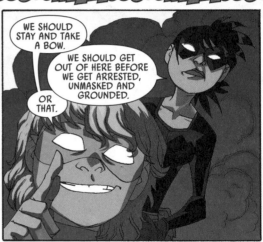

THIS IS- THIS IS EMBARRASSING.

I TOLD YOU!

TOLD ME WHAT??

EEEEOOOOWEEEEOOOOWEEEEOOOOWEEEEOOOOWEEEEOOOO

GET YOUR HANDS ON YOUR HEADS!!

EVERYONE ON THE GROUND.

WE SHOULD STAY AND TAKE A BOW.

WE SHOULD GET OUT OF HERE BEFORE WE GET ARRESTED, UNMASKED AND GROUNDED.

OR THAT.

WHAT WAS *THAT*??

HOW SHOULD I KNOW??

"LADIES AND GENTLEMEN, OUR FIRST GUEST IS THE CUTE HALF OF THE SUPERHERO DUO TAKIO...

"MAKING HER TALK SHOW DEBUT..."

OLIVIA!!

WHAT A THRILL TO BE ON THE SHOW.

OK, FIRST OFF, I AGREED TO COME ON BECAUSE I KNOW A LOT OF PEOPLE ARE SHOCKED, AS ARE WE, TO FIND OUT THERE ARE ACTUAL SUPERHEROES IN THE WORLD.

I KNOW A LOT OF PEOPLE HAVE BEEN HEARING ABOUT US.

A LOT OF PEOPLE WANT TO KNOW HOW WE GOT OUR POWERS...

IF WE ARE FOR REAL.

WELL, IT'S A CRAZY STORY.

OK, SO...

MY SISTER'S BEST FRIEND'S DAD WAS A SCIENTIST AND HE WAS WORKING ON SOME SORT OF INVENTION.

AND SOMETHING WENT WRONG AND WE JUST HAPPENED TO BE AT THEIR HOUSE WHEN ALL THIS CRAZY ENERGY EXPLODED ALL OVER US.

AND WHEN WE WOKE UP WE FOUND OUT WE HAD THESE CRAZY SUPER POWERS.

REAL, HONEST TO GOODNESS, SUPERPOWERS.

NOW THE CRAZY PART, THE PART MY SISTER TAKI DOESN'T LIKE TO TALK ABOUT, IS THAT HER BEST FRIEND, WELL HER EX-BEST FRIEND, KELLY SUE...

SHE WAS THERE TOO.

HEY, HEY, TAKI...

COME SIT WITH US!

HOW COME YOU NEVER SIT WITH US?

I DON'T **NOT** SIT WITH YOU. I WAS–

HEY, I'M ETHAN.

OH, YEAH, I KNOW.

K. COOL. I WASN'T SURE.

SO... ARE YOU AND KELLY SUE NOT SPEAKING?

UH–

THE RUMOR IS YOU'RE, LIKE, BROKEN UP.

I DON'T WANT TO TALK ABOUT ANY OF–

WE THINK SHE HAS SUPERPOWERS.

WE THINK *SHE* WAS ONE OF THE GIRLS IN THE PARKING LOT BLOWING UP THE SCHOOL BUSES.

WITH WHAT?

WITH SUPERPOWERS.

WHAT?

EVERYONE KNOWS.

NO. NO.

THAT'S NOT WHAT HAPPENED.

I SAW IT WITH MY OWN EYES.

YOU DID NOT.

YOU *SAW* KELLY SUE USING SUPERPOWERS?

NO. I SAW GIRLS.

YOU SAW THEIR FACES?

WELL, NO... IT WAS FAR AWAY.

I *KNEW* IT.

I KNOW WHAT I SAW, IZZY.

EXCEPT YOU *DON'T* KNOW WHAT YOU SAW.

LISTEN, I'M GOING TO TELL YOU GUYS SOMETHING BUT YOU CAN'T REPEAT IT...

MY MOM WORKS FOR THE FEDERAL GOVERNMENT, OK? SHE WORKS IN THE FEDERAL COURTHOUSE DOWNTOWN.

SO SHE HEARS A LOT OF STUFF.

AND WHAT REALLY HAPPENED WAS...

SO, LIKE, IT *EXPLODED.*

WHOA!

AND ALL THOSE OTHER EXPLOSIONS WERE JUST, LIKE, CAUSED BY THE ONE GRENADE EXPLODING.

SO IT WAS, LIKE, WHAT YOU CALL...

A CHAIN REACTION.

EXACTLY.

AND THE REASON THEY DIDN'T TELL ANYBODY IS THAT IT'LL MAKE THE F.B.I. DUDES LOOK REALLY, REALLY BAD.

SO THEY, LIKE, COVERED IT UP.

WELL, THAT MAKES A LOT MORE SENSE THAN SUPERPOWERED LITTLE GIRLS.

WHICH *DON'T* EXIST, BY THE WAY.

I *THOUGHT* THAT STORY SOUNDED WEIRD.

IT WAS JUST STUPID.

BRRRIIINGGG

UGH. GEOMETRY.

DID ANYBODY DO THE HOMEWORK?

THE HOMEWORK THAT WAS DUE YESTERDAY?

AND WAS DUE *YESTERDAY?*

SEE YOU IN CLASS!

I KNOW WHAT I SAW.

YOU CAN'T DRAW ATTENTION TO YOURSELF OR PEOPLE ARE GOING TO START PUTTING TWO AND TWO TOGETHER.

AND WHAT WOULD YOU HAVE DONE *BEFORE* YOU GOT POWERS?

THAT GUY WAS *HURTING* THAT GIRL.

UH, CALL A TEACHER OVER?

THEN *THAT'S* WHAT YOU DO NOW.

IT'S JUST HARD TO- TO TURN IT ON AND OFF.

WHAT?

THE *HERO* THING.

IT'S *HARD* TO TURN OFF ONCE YOU'VE TURNED IT ON.

I KNOW.

I WANT TO DO SOMETHING SUPERHEROEY!!

WE SHOULD GO HOME AND DO OUR HOMEWORK.

I DON'T *HAVE* ANY HOMEWORK, TAKI.

THIS *IS* MY HOMEWORK.

WELL, IT'S ALMOST TIME TO HEAD HOME.

IF WE'RE NOT HOME WHEN MOM GETS HOME—

YEAH YEAH...

I JUST WANT TO DO SOMETHING SUPER-COOL AND SUPER-AWESOME AND SUPER—

LISTEN, I TOLD YOU, WE'RE THE ONLY REAL SUPERHEROES ON EARTH.

IT'S NOT LIKE WE CAME WITH A BIG MONSTER ROBOT TO FIGHT.

UGH!! A BIG MONSTER ROBOT WOULD BE *PERFECT.*

IF THERE WAS A BIG MONSTER ROBOT HERE YOU WOULD POOP YOUR TIGHTS.

NUH-UH. *YOU* WOULD.

JUST SAYING *"YOU WOULD"* BACK ISN'T A BURN.

YOU HAVE TO THINK OF SOMETHING FUNNY TO SAY BACK OR DON'T SAY ANYTHING.

YOU DO.

OK, THAT'S IT. WE'RE GOING HOME.

BUT- BUT- BUT- ECH! THIS PLACE IS *FILTHY.* THEY SHOULD *CLEAN* THIS.

PEOPLE AREN'T SUPPOSED TO BE *UP* HERE.

BUT STILL.

AAAAEEEII!!

TAKI!!!

TAKI!?

CAREFUL. CAREFUL, SHE IS ONE OF A KIND.

NOT FOR LONG.

IS THIS HER? TAKI McGILL. AS PROMISED.

THIS IS PATIENT ZERO?

YES, MR. BORGNINE.

WE HAD KELLY SUE BRING HER HERE.

SO NOW IT WILL APPEAR THAT SHE ATTACKED US. BREAKING AND ENTERING.

THE COMPANY WOULD HAVE EVERY RIGHT TO DETAIN HER UNTIL THE AUTHORITIES ARRIVE.

BY THAT TIME WE WILL HAVE WHAT WE NEED FROM HER AND THE PRESS WILL BE SO FOCUSED ON HER *POWERS* THAT-

WHAT ABOUT HER LITTLE SISTER?

WELL, ALL WE REALLY NEED IS HER.

THERE'S NO REASON TO ENDANGER A *SEVEN-YEAR-OLD*.

WE'LL SEE. HURRY UP WITH YOUR EXPERIMENTS, ROTHCHILD.

OBVIOUSLY THIS IS YOUR *LAST CHANCE* TO DO RIGHT BY ME... YOUR LAST CHANCE TO CLEAN THIS MESS UP.

BUT IF YOU DO *RIGHT*, WE WILL ALL BE LOOKING AT A BRAND-NEW DAY IN ADVANCED BIOGENETIC SCIENCES.

AND ALL YOUR PAST SINS WILL BE FORGIVEN.

OOPS! SORRY, TAKI.

OW! COME ON!!

OH, HEY!! IS THIS LUNCH??

I'M STARVIN'.

WHAT'S FOR LUNCH??

STOP IT!!

WAIT, IS THIS PEANUT BUTTER AND JELLY?

I THOUGHT ALL YOUR PEOPLE ATE RICE ALL DAY?

WHO GAVE YOU PERMISSION TO ACT ALL AMERICAN??

WHERE ARE THE NOODLES?? WHERE'S THE GENERAL CHO'S CHICKEN??

NO FORTUNE COOKIE?!! I MEAN, WHAT IS THIS??

SPLING

DUDE, SHE *NAILED* YOU.

I'M GONNA SHOVE THAT BALL UP YOUR BUTT, GOTH PRINCESS!!

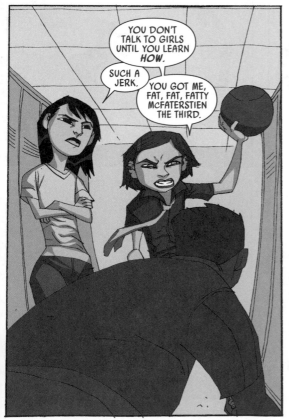

YOU DON'T TALK TO GIRLS UNTIL YOU LEARN *HOW*.

SUCH A JERK.

YOU GOT ME, FAT, FAT, FATTY MCFATERSTIEN THE THIRD.

WHATEVER!!

YEAH, WHATEVER.

YEAH?? AT LEAST I GOT MY REAL PARENTS.

DID, UH, WE JUST FALL, LIKE, OUT OF THE **BUILDING?**

HUH?

I DON'T KNOW ABOUT YOU, I'VE NEVER FALLEN OUT OF A BUILDING BEFORE.

DROP YOUR WEAPONS!!

YOU WILL ALL FEEL THE WRATH OF A SEVEN-YEAR-OLD-

UH...

OH, **COME ON!**

OH, COME ON!!

I HAD **DOUBLE SUPERPOWERS!!**

I CAN'T GO BACK TO JUST **NORMAL** SUPERPOWERS AFTER I HAD **DOUBLE SUPERPOWERS!!**

OLIVIA??

I THOUGHT WE WERE GOING TO THE POLICE.

WHAT'S TO THINK ABOUT?

YOU WERE STRAPPED TO A TABLE AND THEY WERE ABOUT TO PULL OUT YOUR BRAIN.

I DON'T KNOW WHAT TO DO.

THEY ARE *BAD GUYS.*

THEY ARE.

LET'S GO TELL MOM.

YOU'RE RIGHT.

I'M ALWAYS RIGHT.

YOU ARE ALMOST NEVER RIGHT.

I WAS RIGHT TO COME SAVE YOU.

(ALL STRAPPED TO THE TABLE.)

THANK YOU.

SAY IT.

YOU'RE THE BEST SUPERHERO IN THE WORLD.

MOM?

SHE'S ASLEEP.

WE INTERRUPT OUR REGULARLY SCHEDULED PROGRAM FOR THIS CHANNEL 3 EXCLUSIVE!

WE ARE BROADCASTING TO YOU LIVE FROM GRESHAM COUNTY AND THE HEADQUARTERS OF THE CHEMICAL CONGLOMERATE KNOWN AS GLOBOSURGE INDUSTRIES...

WHERE WE HAVE BEEN TOLD THAT THE POLICE HAVE INTERACTED WITH A YOUNG GIRL WHO MULTIPLE WITNESSES, INCLUDING POLICE OFFICERS, NOW SAY SHOWED EVIDENCE OF WHAT CAN ONLY BE DESCRIBED AS SUPERPOWERS!

THERE HAVE BEEN NUMEROUS REPORTS IN THE MEDIA OF SUPERPOWERED CHILDREN ALL OVER THE CITY, BUT WE HAVE NOT HAD **OFFICIAL CONFIRMATION** OR A SIGHTING FROM SOMEONE OF AUTHORITY.

UNTIL NOW.

POLICE WERE CALLED AFTER NUMEROUS DISTURBANCES— WHAT WAS DESCRIBED AS SOUNDS OF EXPLOSIONS.

IT WAS THIS— THIS GIRL.

SHE SAID HER NAME WAS KELLY OR KATIE AND SHE SAID THAT SHE WAS THE GIRL WE KEEP HEARING ABOUT ONLINE.

WE DIDN'T BELIEVE HER BUT SHE— SHE UP AND FLEW AWAY.

NOW I'M TELLING YOU WHAT I SAW— WHAT WE ALL SAW I HAVE NEVER SEEN IN MY **ENTIRE LIFE.**

YOU SPOKE TO HER? YOU SPOKE TO HER DIRECTLY?

I SPOKE TO HER AND SHE CONFESSED THAT HER FATHER HAD ACCIDENTALLY TURNED HER INTO A SUPERPOWERED PERSON AND THAT THE PEOPLE AT THIS COMPANY TRIED TO KIDNAP HER HERE AND THEN SHE FOUGHT THEM OFF.

THEN SHE JUST FLEW AWAY.

SHE FLEW?

IF NO ONE KNOWS WE WERE THERE AND THE BAD GUY LEFT THE COUNTRY...

WHAT ABOUT KELLY SUE'S EVIL DAD?

IF HE TELLS THEM ABOUT US, HE GETS IN **MORE** TROUBLE.

IF ANY OF THEM TELLS ANYBODY ABOUT US THEY GET IN CRAZY TROUBLE.

SO KELLY REALLY HELPED US OUT HERE?

WOW.

REALLY WOW.

NO OFFENSE TO THE ARRESTING OFFICERS, WHO I AM SURE ARE FINE MEN, BUT SUPERPOWERED LITTLE KIDS?

WE MAKE DEODORANT AND SHAMPOO.

WITHOUT PHYSICAL PROOF THIS SEEMS TO HAVE HOAX WRITTEN ALL OVER IT.

HOAX? EVEN BETTER.

WHAT'S EVEN BETTER?

COVER UP. THEY ARE TRYING TO COVER IT UP.

WHAT DOES THAT MEAN?

THEY CAN'T **ADMIT** THAT WE **EXIST** OR **THEY** ARE IN TROUBLE.

IS THIS GOOD?

THIS IS **VERY** GOOD.

THIS DID NOT GO THE WAY I **THOUGHT** IT WAS GOING TO GO.

SHOULD WE STILL TELL MOM?

NO MORE TUSHY BURPING IN THE BED... SNORT.

LET'S NOT.

WHAT?!! WHAT DO YOU *WANT*??

YOU WANT TO *FIGHT*?? I'M NOT AFRAID OF YOU!!

I CAME TO SAY I'M SORRY.

GO AWAY.

I KNOW YOU *HATE* ME NOW.

I HATE ME NOW TOO.

YOU HAVE *NO IDEA* WHAT THIS HAS BEEN LIKE. TO WAKE UP ONE DAY AND REALIZE YOUR DAD IS- IS- IS JUST AWFUL.

HE'S AWFUL AND HE'S ALL I HAVE.

EXCEPT NOW HE'S IN JAIL SO I DON'T HAVE *HIM* ANYMORE EITHER.

I JUST CAME TO SAY... I'M SORRY.

I *REALLY* AM.

I DON'T *BELIEVE* YOU.

AS OF THIS MORNING, ONLY 22% OF OUR VIEWERS BELIEVE THAT THERE IS SUCH A THING AS A SUPERPOWERED CHILD.

WHERE IS MOM?

SCHOOL.

WHY IS OUR MOM AT SCHOOL AND NOT US?

PARENT-TEACHER CONFERENCE.

WE DON'T HAVE SCHOOL.

WE DON'T HAVE SCHOOL?

SO... WE DON'T HAVE ANYTHING TO DO ALL DAY.

MAYBE WE SHOULD GO... PATROLLING?

IS THAT WHAT YOU CALL IT?

WHEN SUPERHEROES GO LOOKING AROUND FOR GOOD THINGS TO DO?

THAT IS EXACTLY WHAT YOU CALL IT!!

I'M GOING TO GO GET MY COSTUME!!

HEY, OLIVIA.

WHAT?

I'M SORRY I DIDN'T BRING YOU ALONG TO THAT THING.

WE'RE PARTNERS.

I'LL NEVER DO THAT AGAIN.

IT'S YOU AND ME.

THE END

COVER GALLERY

TAKIO #1

TAKIO #2

TAKIO #3

TAKIO #4

SKETCH BOOK

Layout & Final Art #4, Page 5

Layout & Final Art #4, Pages 7-8

Layout & Final Art #4, Pages 9-10